Introduction to
Google
Classroom

Annie Brock

Introduction to
Google
Classroom

A Practical Guide for:
» **Implementing Digital Education Strategies**
» **Creating Engaging Classroom Activities**
» **Building an Effective Online Learning Environment**

Fully Revised & Updated Edition

⊛ ULYSSES PRESS

Published in the United States by:
Ulysses Press
P.O. Box 3440
Berkeley, CA 94703
www.ulyssespress.com

ISBN: 978-1-64604-165-7

Printed in Canada by Marquis Book Printing
10 9 8 7 6 5 4 3 2 1

Acquisitions editor: Ashten Evans
Managing editor: Claire Chun
Editor: Scott Calamar
Proofreader: Renee Rutledge
Front cover and interior design/layout: what!design @ whatweb.com
Cover illustrations: © Freud/shutterstock.com

Contents

Part 1

The Google Classroom Advantage

As a twenty-first century teacher, you are facing a set of opportunities and challenges that no other teachers in the history of education have encountered. In the last ten years, an explosion of technology has radically changed the educational landscape. This technology has brought with it incredible benefits like more efficient communication, better access to knowledge and resources, and increased student engagement. But because of its relative newness, it's likely your pre-service teaching program did not adequately prepare you to effectively use technology as part of your teaching repertoire.

Today's teachers are poised to change both teaching and learning through integration of technology in the classroom. The business sector thrives on technology—in fact, many of the world's largest companies, like Apple, Microsoft, and Google, produce it. The world has seen massive globalization thanks to the newfound ability to communicate instantaneously across the planet. Just as technology has transformed the way you live, it has the capacity to transform the way you teach. As the paradigm shifts in other industries, emerging technologies are also offering powerful alternatives to traditional methods of education. Despite these advancements, however, many of today's classrooms look virtually identical to the classrooms of fifty years ago.

Utilizing technology in new and interesting ways in the classroom isn't just important to keeping your teaching style fresh and relevant, it's essential experience for your students who will one day venture out to work and live in this technologically driven world.

Blended learning is the practice of combining face-to-face instruction with online learning experiences. Many school districts are encouraging teachers to incorporate blended learning techniques into the traditional classroom model, in an effort to provide students with a more diverse educational experience. No longer are your students limited to learning only what you know or what the textbook says; rather, they have a limitless amount of information at their fingertips. Thus, the goal of teaching should not only be to impart knowledge, but also to assist students in effectively seeking it out for themselves. In the blended learning model, the teacher acts as a facilitator who guides students to ensure that they access new information in a safe, responsible, and purposeful manner.

As we consider ways to meaningfully incorporate technology in our classrooms, there is no better place to begin than Google's G Suite for Education. You undoubtedly already have a handle on what it means to "google." After all, the company's powerful search engine is the most popular in the world. However, Google has also developed a sophisticated suite of productivity tools and made them available, free of charge, to schools around the globe.

From Gmail (Google's popular email service) to a host of other products like Google Docs (a word processing program), Google Calendar (an electronic scheduling and calendar solution), and Google Drive (a cloud storage service), Google's suite of communication-driven tools allows teachers and students alike to work smarter. Collaboration is king when it comes to Google for Education (GFE). No longer do meaningful learning experiences have to be bound by the four walls of your classroom. Using G Suite for Education, students can work collaboratively with you and each other and access information any time from any device.

For K–12 educators, the built-in creativity, productivity, and communication tools, increased efficiency, and cost-saving capabilities offered by Google provide an incredible opportunity to meet digital natives where they are and prepare them for life in the modern world. No single tool in the suite is better suited to meeting educational needs than Google Classroom.

At its most basic level, Google Classroom is an app that helps teachers easily and efficiently assign, collect, and return work to students. Of course, you could simply replace these once-analog processes with their digital counterparts, but truly harnessing the power of Google Classroom creates an opportunity to do much more. Classroom can serve as the foundation of your blended learning integration strategy. Google refers to Classroom as "mission control" for your classes; used purposefully, it can be the touchstone for all of the online learning your students will do throughout the year.

You likely already have a system in place to accomplish the tasks of assigning and returning work to students, so why replace that system with Google Classroom? Sure, it can streamline your workflow process, but utilizing Classroom can also enhance your ability to communicate with students, differentiate instruction, and share new concepts and tools in real time. Embedded in the fabric of Google Classroom are new ideas and approaches to education. The focus on a partnership between students and teachers, the tools to access and disseminate valuable information in real time, and the ability to evaluate student progress and give instantaneous feedback make Classroom a game changer.

Aside from these larger implications, Classroom can also impact simple tasks and minor issues by helping to prevent them from becoming major headaches.

Imagine receiving this email:

> To: Ms. Brock
> From: Frustrated Parent
> Re: Sam's Essay
>
> Dear Ms. Brock,
>
> Sam told me he turned in his essay on time and you docked him 10 percent for it being "late." Can you explain this?
>
> Thanks,
>
> Frustrated Parent

You've probably received an email or phone message resembling this one—an annoyed parent pointing out a discrepancy with the grade you've given and the one they believe their child has earned. This can be a source of irritation for both teachers and parents. But now imagine being able to simply respond with this:

Dear Frustrated Parent,

Attached you will find a time-stamped screenshot showing when Sam uploaded his assignment; it was submitted at 9:17 p.m. on Thursday night—unfortunately, it was due the prior Monday morning. I understand Sam has a lot going on, but if he's unsure about due dates in the future, our class syllabus and calendar can be accessed 24/7 via our Google Classroom. Please let me know if you have further questions!

Ms. Brock

Or imagine receiving this note:

Ms. Brock,

I was out sick Monday, Tuesday, and Wednesday. What did I miss?

Stephanie

These types of requests can be exasperating for a teacher. Consider the time it takes to stop what you're doing and look back through lesson plans and calendars to figure out exactly what a student missed, not to mention the time required to gather the necessary resources for makeup work. Now, multiply that by the number of absences in your class every year. Think of how much time it could save you to be able to respond like this:

Stephanie,

All lessons, readings, and assignments are posted on our Google Classroom. Scroll down to locate the dates you were absent and complete the work as indicated. Email me if you need any clarification. Hope you're feeling better!

Ms. Brock

Google Classroom may not be the cure for every common teaching headache, but the paper trail it leaves behind can be invaluable. Think of the hundreds of times you have had to stop what you were doing and look back at old paperwork to solve problems or retrieve information for individual students. Google Classroom has the potential to alleviate common organizational problems that plague teachers.

So, who can use Google Classroom? Many mistakenly believe it is limited to middle and high school students and teachers, but it has a place in elementary schools as well. Truly, if your students can master the art of logging in, they can use Classroom. As with all educational tools, modification is key. Start slow and figure out how to best use Classroom with your students. A first grade teacher may simply post a link to a primary-friendly online spelling game. A third grade teacher may post a question and ask students to answer it, and then ask them to respond to one another's comments. A high school teacher may use Classroom as an exclusive portal for collecting and grading assignments. No matter how you put Google Classroom to work, it has applications at every level of education. The sooner students learn how to operate competently in the digital realm, the better.

The Benefits of Google Classroom

There are many advantages to using Google Classroom, but let's talk about some of the most beneficial reasons you should make the leap sooner rather than later. Google Classroom helps you:

Go paperless. At some point in your career, an administrator has probably encouraged you to use less paper, and rightly so. Paper, ink, and toner are costly consumables that school districts must constantly replace. The costs associated with purchasing and maintaining copy machines can quickly eat away at thinly stretched budgets. In addition, using large quantities of paper has environmental consequences. Google touts the paperless nature of Classroom's workflow as one of its primary advantages. Think about how much paper is wasted in your class each year, and consider whether or not it's a necessary or thoughtful use of those resources. Taking your classroom digital means using less paper, which is good for everyone.

Reduce student organization problems. Using Google Classroom means both in-progress and completed work are in a single place. We've all seen it before: a bewildered and frustrated student riffling through an unkempt backpack or locker, desperately trying to find a missing page of homework. Utilizing Google Classroom means students always know where to find their work. Everything is automatically stored in a file on Google Drive. With easy-to-use search options and intuitive folder organization, it's rare for something to get lost. The students' work is safely tucked away as soon as it's created. In addition, since Google tools automatically save with every keystroke and provide a revision history, they make it nearly impossible to accidentally delete something. Everything is right there in the cloud.

...And teacher organization problems. Disorganization isn't exclusive to students; teachers can lose things, too! Sure, there are those who might have a perfectly maintained color-coded filing system, but most teachers have a few chinks in their organizational armor. Keeping track of late work and makeup work is enough to throw even the most organized teachers for a loop. Using Google Classroom, you can set clear due dates and have an up-to-the-minute record of all the work that has been turned in. Plus, Classroom automatically stores everything in Google Drive, so copies of every original assignment and all student work are kept in Google Drive folders. If anything goes wrong, it's a simple process to go back, find the problem, and make it right.

Evaluate better. Because a copy of student work is saved in Google Drive, teachers effectively have a built-in system for storing everything a student does throughout the term. This system can be used in a variety of creative ways. At the end of the year, you could help students select their best work for a portfolio. Or, you might share a few projects from a student's file with curious parents at a conference. A student with an IEP (Individualized Education Program) or specific learning goals can have a clear record of work from which you and other educational professionals evaluate progress. These files may prove invaluable when determining new educational goals or implementing instructional scaffolding, a process based on tailoring learning to each student's needs and goals. There is no end to the potential uses of an on-demand record of every student's work.

Talk more. Google Classroom allows for a constant two-way stream of communication between students and teachers. You can use the Classroom stream to post announcements on which students can comment, or pose questions for them to answer. Even students who were absent from school can get in on a discussion. There is an opportunity to leave remarks and send comments to students at nearly every phase of the workflow process. As most teachers know, leaving lengthy comments on paper-based student work takes time and often results in some serious hand cramping, but utilizing the communication features in Google Classroom is far less time consuming (and completely cramp free). A lot of student communication in their private lives is done electronically, so they are adept at communicating in this manner and appreciative when you take the time to send a digital note or comment. It doesn't have to be in red ink to mean something.

For these reasons and so many more, Google Classroom can be a game changer for an educator. The innumerable ways this digital portal can open the doors to our physical classrooms 24/7 can make a significant impact on the student learning process. The increased opportunities for communication with students can positively impact accountability and engagement. In addition, using technological tools in the classroom offers students experiential learning in this new domain.

It is critical for today's students to become literate in responsible technology use. Already, students manage many of their relationships online, and as we've seen, this can result in some irreversible, life-changing missteps. Bringing technology into the classroom, modeling its responsible use, and guiding students as they use it in real-world scenarios will provide them with the experience and know-how they need to avoid online fiascoes in the future.

Of course, Google Classroom should not be the sole mode of interaction with students. No matter how sophisticated a tool Classroom may be, it is still just a tool. Technology cannot replace meaningful student-teacher relationships, but with commitment and ingenuity, it has the potential to make those relationships even stronger.

Part 2

A Step-by-Step Guide to Using Google Classroom

Logging In and Creating a Class

Before you get started learning how to use Google Classroom, there are a few pieces of background information you need to know. Google Classroom is accessible to students and staff of schools enrolled in the Google for Education program. If you are unsure whether or not your school has a GFE account, contact your technology director or support personnel for confirmation.

Your school's GFE administrator has access to a dashboard where all users are assigned either a student or teacher role in Google Classroom. Teachers are able to create classes, whereas students are only allowed to join them (unless given a special designation by the dashboard administrator).

To log in:

1. Go to www.classroom.google.com.

2. Log in with your school credentials (i.e., the same username and password you use to access your email account).

3. The first time logging in, you will be asked to identify whether you are a teacher or student. It is very important that you clarify your status as a teacher at this step. If you inadvertently select Student and find that you are unable to create a class in Google Classroom, contact your GFE administrator to correct your status in the administrator dashboard.

If you're new to any of the other Google education apps, like Gmail, Google Docs, or Google Drive, you'll want to familiarize yourself with all three. These applications work together with Classroom to create a seamless communication and workflow process: Google Classroom depends on Gmail for communication, Docs for content creation, and Drive for storage. If you've never used any of these apps before, do not panic.

A helpful tip for new users is to associate the G Suite for Education tools with familiar counterparts. For example, think of Google Docs as a counterpart to Microsoft Word. Google Docs is a word processing program just like Microsoft Word—with the addition of built-in communication tools that increase its functionality for teachers. Gmail is an email program similar to Outlook, Yahoo!, and other email systems you've likely used in the past. Google Drive is similar to the hard drive on your computer (or you could even say it's like a filing cabinet!), except instead of keeping your files locally, Drive stores them in the cloud.

Storing something in "the cloud" simply means that instead of saving it locally to your desktop or a flash drive, you're enlisting the help of a remote storage service and its servers to store it on your behalf. There are several examples of cloud services in addition to Google, such as iCloud and Dropbox. Once it's saved on their servers, you can retrieve your data through a web browser or app from any device, anywhere, anytime. While many cloud storage services cost money, Google offers GFE users unlimited storage space for free.

Later, we'll talk more about how the other Google for Education apps interact with Google Classroom to create a streamlined, paperless assignment flow between you and your students. For now, you've logged into Google Classroom and identified yourself as a teacher, so next we'll create a class.

Creating a class in Google Classroom is as easy as clicking a button. In fact, that really is all you have to do—click a button! In the top right corner of your Google Classroom home screen, next to your email address or avatar, you'll see a plus-sign icon. Click here and two options will appear: "Join class" and "Create class." Click the Create option and a pop-up box will appear, asking you 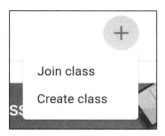 to enter some details about your class, including the "Class name," Section, Subject, and "Room number." The only required information is your class name, but you have the option to enter more information to help you and your students stay organized. Once you enter the class name and any other information, click Create in the bottom right corner of the pop-up box. You've created your first Google Classroom—just like that. Now, let's go make it yours!

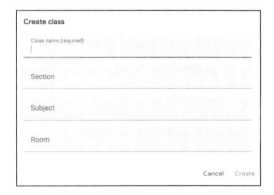

Getting Acquainted with Google Classroom

You'll be taken into your Google Classroom as soon as it's created. It will look bare bones at first, but don't worry; soon, it will be fully customized and ready to populate with content for your students. As you enter your classroom, you'll see a message that reads, "What's new in Classroom." This box will detail features that have been added to Google Classroom most recently. These are important to note because Classroom is updating and adding new features all the time. Click "Got it" when you're ready.

Again, your Google Classroom will look pretty sparse in the beginning stages, so let's take a quick dime tour of your new classroom to draw attention to some key features that will be important as you use the app.

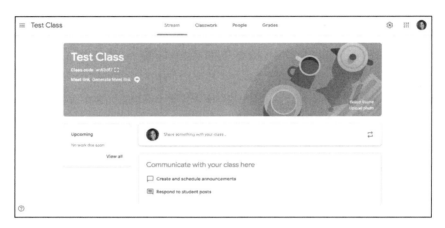

At the top of the screen you will see a menu with four items: Stream, Classwork, People, and Grades. You will use these four categories to navigate around your classroom. On the main page of your classroom you will also see a header with a generated theme. (We'll talk about how to customize this on page 18.) Note that in the header, you will see a "Class code." Your unique class code is like a secret knock for entering your classroom. Simply share the number and letter code with your students so that they may join your classroom. If you click the display icon next to your class code, you can enlarge it so students can better see it via a projector or your screen. We'll discuss the class code in detail later on, but for now it's important to know that it is case sensitive, meaning your students must enter the code exactly as it appears in order to be admitted to your classroom. Under the class code you will see text that reads: "Meet link Generate Meet link." A "Meet link" allows you to create a video-based meeting space with your students through your Google Classroom. Using Google Meet in conjunction with your classroom is especially helpful for distance learning. To set up the link, simply click "Generate Meet link," and a pop-up will appear with the address of your Meet link. Click Save and your Meet link will appear in the header. The Meet link will not change unless you change it.

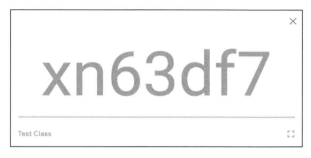

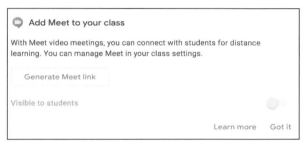

On the left side of the screen in the body of the classroom, you will see an Upcoming vertical menu. This will list all the work that is due soon. This area will begin to populate as you create new assignments. They will be listed in the order of the due dates given. In the main body of the screen, there are two boxes. One is a text box that will feature your avatar, and a smaller text box. Simply navigate to the area that says "Share something with your class...," and start typing. This will create an announcement you can share with the class. (We'll talk more about this on page 34.) Finally, there is a section that says "Communicate with your class here." This is the area where your announcements, assignments, and posts will show up; it is called the "Stream." Everything you post will appear here in the order it is posted (newest posts will be listed first).

Customizing Your Classroom

Many teachers spend their summers carefully selecting décor and laboring over bulletin boards to improve the look and feel of their real-life classroom. After all, it's well documented that inviting, personalized spaces help students feel more comfortable and prepared to learn. For the same reason, you'll want to take some time to personalize your Google Classroom. Giving Google Classroom some of your unique flair reminds students that this virtual space is deeply intertwined with your physical classroom, and that the same rules and expectations apply.

There are two options for customizing the look of your Google Classroom. In the bottom right corner of the header image, you will see two buttons: "Select theme" and "Upload photo."

Selecting a Theme

Choosing "Select theme" will initiate a pop-up gallery window. The gallery offers a bank of preselected images organized by subject matter including General, English & History, Math & Science, Art, Sports, and Other. Browse these to find an image that pairs well with your discipline. There are lots of images to choose from, and they address a variety of content 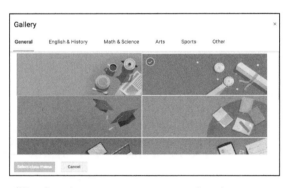 areas, as well as more general education themes (like books, computers, graduation caps, etc.).

Once you find the image you like, simply click on it. A check mark will appear in the upper-left corner of the thumbnail you've selected. Click the "Select class theme" button at the bottom of the window to choose the image you've selected as the header image.

Uploading a Photo

By choosing "Upload photo," you will be able to add a custom photo or image to the header. You might make the header image a shot of your desk or a picture of your students to connect the virtual classroom with the physical one. If your physical classroom has a theme, like Ms. V's Superhero Students, consider extending it to your virtual classroom. The header image can be changed

at any time, so you can even regularly update it to reflect each new unit of study. If your students are members of multiple Google Classrooms, this personalization tactic will also help remind them of which class they have entered in the virtual realm.

Once you've uploaded or selected an image for your classroom, it will appear in the header. Since you can change this going forward, choose a placeholder and revisit it later if you can't decide just yet.

Class Settings—Class Details

Above the header image you've chosen, note a cog icon that will lead you to your Class Settings. Here you can set various details of your class. Clicking the icon will take you to a page with three sections—Class Details, General, and Grading. In the Class Details section, you can edit any of the information that you originally listed when creating the class, including the "Class name,"

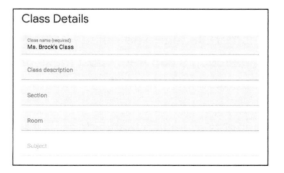

"Class description," Section, Room, and Subject. Try to be specific here; instead of entering just "English," try using "Ms. Brock's English Class" or "Sophomore Honors English." The next line offers an opportunity to describe the class in more detail, including a brief synopsis of the class or class objectives. The line labeled "Room," asks, "Where does the class meet?" In this space, in addition to entering your room number, consider adding the days and times your class meets (e.g., Blue Days, 2nd Period, or M–W–F from 8:00 a.m. to 9:00 a.m., etc.). The more details you can provide here, the better.

Class Settings—General

In the General section, you can make several settings adjustments. You can reset your class code in this space. Your class code is visible in this box, which includes a drop-drown menu featuring four items: Display, Copy, Reset, and Disable. You may want to reset your class code for a variety of reasons. Perhaps it has a zero, and you're afraid students will confuse it with a capital O. Maybe you're concerned an unauthorized user has attempted to join using the code. Whatever the reason, you can reset the class code as many times as necessary. You can also disable the code altogether and restrict student entry to invitation only.

The next line, Stream, asks you to set permissions for who is able to post on the classroom. You can choose different posting options by clicking the drop-down box. "Posting" refers to your students' ability to share messages and content on the main Google Classroom Stream, while "commenting" refers to their ability to respond to posts put up by you or another student. The default setting is "Students can post and comment," which means that students can freely post messages and reply to and comment on others' posts. If you allow students the ability to post, they will see a plus sign in the bottom right corner of the page when viewing the class stream. This option allows students the ability not only to post thoughts, questions, and ideas, but also to share multimedia content.

Allowing students to post and comment increases the communication function of Google Classroom. Picture a panicked student posting this announcement the night before a big test: "Help! Can someone explain the checks and balances system to me again? I'm so confused!" Teachers and fellow students would be able to answer that student's call for help and provide them with information when they need it most. A twenty-four-hour service like Google Classroom means that questions no longer have to wait until tomorrow, or, worse yet, go unanswered altogether.

In this capacity, your classroom can be its own little social networking site. With the benefits of constant communication, however, come drawbacks. If you choose to provide your students with these communication tools, it is important to also set expectations and guidelines for using them.

The second option, "Students can only comment," gives students permission to reply to or comment on things you have posted, but not to initiate messages or post their own content. Allowing students to comment but not post is a great way to encourage discussion while still controlling the classroom's content. Think of how many times you have seen people contribute diverse opinions to an interesting Facebook status. Posting a food-for-thought item, such as a video clip or provocative question, and asking students to comment on it is a great way to initiate discussion on a topic you are introducing in class. By the same token, we've all seen conversations like this go awry. Perhaps an argument breaks out, or an incident of cyberbullying or inappropriateness takes place. As the teacher, you have the ability to delete any posts or comments added by a student.

The final option, "Only teacher can post or comment," prevents students from posting and commenting altogether. If this setting suits your needs, then by all means choose it. Keep in mind, however, that allowing students the opportunity to contribute to the conversation has the potential to strengthen both student-to-teacher and student-to-student communication, as well as overall student engagement.

The next line is "Classwork on the stream." In this area you can decide whether the classwork you assign will show up as a condensed notification on the screen with all the attachments and details, which then requires students to click through for more details, or whether to hide classwork notifications altogether. The setting defaults to "Show condensed notifications," which shares information, but keeps your stream from getting too bogged down with information.

The following line in the General section is "Show deleted items." This is for teacher use only. It's a decision whether or not to see all content, even the content that you have deleted. It defaults to being turned off, but you can toggle the switch to turn on this setting if you want to continue seeing assignments/posts that you have deleted.

The final line regards your Google Meet link. Here you can copy the link to paste it in an announcement or email or to invite someone from outside the class to join your online discussion. You can also reset the link if someone whom you prefer not have access to your online meetings has gained access to the link. You can also toggle on and off the Meet link's visibility to the students, if you prefer to keep it private and only share when necessary. You can always keep the same Google Meet link, or you can change it as often as you like.

Class Settings—Grading

The final section of the Class Settings page is Grading. In this section, you can determine how grades are calculated and displayed. Under the subheading "Grade calculation," you can choose your grading calculation system by clicking the drop-down box. There are choices for "No overall grade," "Total points," and "Weighted by category." You might choose "No overall grade" if you only want to grade individual assignments but not keep a running tally of students' grades. If, for example, you use a program like PowerSchool to keep track of overall grades, you would likely choose this option. You can also choose "Total points," which will keep a running grade based on overall points—in this scenario all assignments are given the same weight toward the total grade. The final choice is "Weighted by category." This would be appropriate to choose if you want to keep running grade totals in your Google Classroom but want different assignments like tests and essays to count more toward the final grade than other daily assignments. (We'll talk about how to set up categories in a moment.)

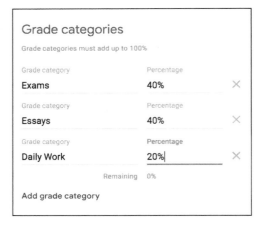

The next line is "Show overall grade to students." Here you can toggle on and off the students' ability to see their running overall grade.

The last subheading in this section is "Grade categories." If you have chosen to weight grades based on categories, you'll want to enter that information in here. Simply click "Add grade category" and choose your categories and what weighted percentage they will have toward the overall grade. The percentages you choose must add up to 100 percent.

Once you've made the appropriate changes to your class settings, simply click the Save button in the top right corner to save your settings. You may change these as frequently as you like until you find the right settings that work for your Google Classroom.

Accessing the Classroom Drive Folder

Another feature of the main page is the "hamburger button," called this because the three horizontal lines bear a resemblance to a hamburger. Clicking this icon will bring up a vertical menu along the left side of your screen. From here, you can access all your classes on the home page of your Google Classroom account by clicking the Classes link.

Classes

When you click the Classes link, each one of your classes will appear as a separate box in your Google Classroom dashboard. This is the page you will see when you log into Classroom each day. Please notice that there are a few options that you can access for each class. The arrow icon at the bottom of each class box will take you to the grade book for that class. The folder icon will take you to the Google Drive folder for that class. Google Classroom automatically generates this Google Drive folder to store all assignments

and student work added to your classroom. It's like having a filing cabinet that fills itself! Clicking the folder icon opens Google Drive in a new window, where you'll see that the folder is currently empty. Don't worry; it will fill up fast when you start adding assignments. We will discuss how to use the Google Drive folder later, but for now there's one very important thing to know: DO NOT DELETE THE FOLDER. Deleting the folder will cause you a lot of headaches later on, so it's important to leave it be for now.

In each box on the home screen, you'll see the title of a class you have created or in which you are enrolled. For any class you have created, you can click the three vertical dots in the upper-right corner of its box. This gives you a drop-down menu that allows you to either move, edit, copy, or archive the class. Clicking move will allow you to rearrange the order of your classes as they appear on your home screen. Clicking Edit will result in a pop-up that allows you to change the basic details of the class, clicking Copy will create a duplicate of the class that you can rename, and clicking Archive will put the class in your archive folder when you are done using it so that it will no longer appear on your home screen.

The next item on the menu is Calendar. Clicking this link will take you to a weekly calendar within the Classroom app that displays upcoming due dates. This calendar will automatically populate each time you add a due date to your classroom to help both teachers and students keep track of upcoming assignments.

Google Classroom generates an individual in-app calendar for each class, but you can also access a master calendar that displays due dates for all of your classes. When you choose Calendar from the menu, you'll be taken to a color-coded calendar that shows which assignments are due when in your various classrooms. You will automatically start on the current week, but you can use the arrows at the top of the page to navigate to different weeks. Clicking a colored assignment block on the calendar will take you to a page that shows data and details associated with that assignment. In Student View, when a student clicks on a colored block, they will be taken straight to a page where they can turn in the assignment. There is a drop-down menu labeled "All Classes" at the top-left corner of the calendar displaying all your classes; this allows you to toggle from the master calendar to the calendar of a specific class.

Both an in-app Classroom calendar and a Google Calendar are created when you make your Google Classroom. As you add assignments with due dates to your Google Classroom, those dates will automatically appear on these two calendars.

The next section you find has a Teaching subhead. Under this there are two options, To-do and Test Class. Clicking the To-do link will take you to a page where you can review student work. There are two menu items at the top of this page: "To review" and "Reviewed." In the "To review" area, you'll see work that has been submitted by students that you have yet to review and return. You can find work that you have returned in the Reviewed section. Note a drop-down menu toward the top left of this page. Here you can choose whether to see work to review for all your classes or just a single class. Clicking the name of your class in the Teaching area of the menu will navigate you to the stream page of any of your classrooms.

Archived Classes

If you have archived any classes that you are no longer teaching, you can access them by clicking on the Archived Classes link. This will take you to a page with all your inactive classes so that you may access them. If you have archived a class, you must restore it before you can add anything to it or edit it in any way. Simply open the class and click Restore at the bottom to do this.

Settings

The last item on this menu is Settings. This is different from your class settings. Clicking this brings you to a page that can help you manage the settings for your Google account and for your classroom in particular.

Profile

The first section of this page is Profile. Here you can change your profile picture. You can upload an image from your computer or use any image on your Google Drive as your profile picture. You can also alter any of your chosen account settings. Clicking Manage under Account Settings lets you fine-tune the choices currently applied to your overall Google account profile. These settings include, among others, updating your password and other security options like adding secondary contact information, such as a cell phone number.

Notifications

Also on the Settings page is a section titled "Notifications," which allows the user to check or uncheck a box labeled "Receive email notifications." By default, Google Classroom notifications will be turned on. This is true for both students and teachers. It is highly recommended that students keep them turned on so that reminders of upcoming due dates and teacher feedback can be delivered directly to their email inboxes. If students are using the mobile version of Google

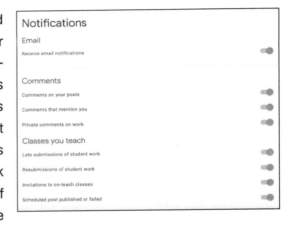

Classroom with either an Android or iOS device, they will also have the opportunity to enable mobile notifications. If so, these push notifications will appear on their electronic device whenever a student or teacher responds to their posts, mentions them in a comment, or sends them a direct message. A student may check Google Classroom often enough so they don't need notifications to be reminded of assignments to complete and questions to answer. Some students prefer to check each of their classroom courses at specific times of the day when they can immediately address any new developments. Other students may want notifications to keep them apprised of updates and messages from the teacher.

Teachers may not want to receive email notifications whenever a student turns in an assignment or posts a comment, as it can lead to a deluge in your inbox. Just toggle to turn notifications on or off, depending on your preference. Many social networks offer notifications when someone tags you, mentions you, or posts something to your wall. Receiving too many messages becomes annoying and cumbersome to sift through. Just know that you can change your notifications settings any time. You can also choose which notifications you want to receive.

The next subheading in the Notifications section is Comments. Here you can choose whether or not to receive a notification when someone comments on your post, makes a comment that specifically mentions you, or when you receive a private comment on a student's work. You can also customize your notifications under the "Classes you teach" subheading by choosing whether or not to receive notifications when late work is turned in, when student work is resubmitted, when you are invited to co-teach a class, or when your scheduled posts are published or if they fail to publish. You make these decisions by using the toggle buttons next to each item. Under "Class notifications" you can completely turn off all email and mobile notifications by toggling the button next to the class you would like to turn on or off.

The Question Mark Icon

Before we discuss how to start posting on the stream, you might have noticed a small question mark icon in the lower-left corner of the screen. When you click the question mark, you are given a menu with four options: "What's new," "Report issue or request feature," "Help Center," and "Help Community."

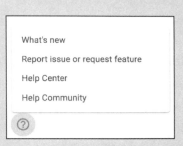

- **What's New.** This links to a page on Google's support site listing the new features they've added to Classroom. Check here often, as new features are being added all the time, especially in these early stages.

- **Report issue or request feature.** This option allows you to initiate a message to Google. Google encourages its users to send feedback regarding problems or issues, share ideas for new features that would enhance the product, and offer general reviews about experiences with the app. Teachers and students should take advantage of this feature, as Google is known to improve its products and add new features based on user feedback.

- **Help Center and Help Community.** The final two items on the question mark icon's menu direct you to the Google Classroom Help Center and the Help Community. The Help Center will offer you step-by-step instructions on how to use different features of Classroom or lead you through common troubleshooting issues. The Help Center guidance is provided by the Google Classroom team. The Help Community allows you to ask and answer questions among the Google Classroom community. These answers and posts are user-generated, but they may link back to Google's Help Center instructions. Just remember, the Help Center provides help from Google; the Help Community provides answers crowdsourced from other Google Classroom users.

Now that you've familiarized yourself with the basics of your stream, we're going to examine the People tab before we start posting.

People Tab: Adding and Managing Students

After filling in all the general information about the class, it's time to populate your Google Classroom with students. Make sure your Classroom's theme and information are organized so that you are prepared for students to enter. You wouldn't want students walking into a disheveled room on the first day of school, and the same logic should apply to your virtual classroom. Make all necessary preparations before inviting students in. When you're ready, click the People tab in the menu and you will be taken to a page that looks like this:

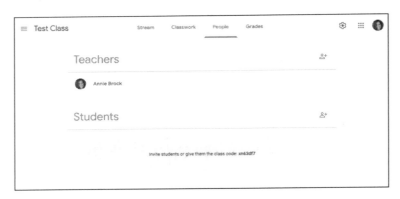

You'll note this page is relatively empty at first, but it will soon hold the roster of all the students enrolled in the class, along with any co-teachers. There are two sections on this page: Teachers and Students. In the Teachers section, you will see your name and profile picture, as well as a person icon with a plus sign. This is your Invite icon. Simply type the name of a teacher you'd like to invite and, once the invitation is accepted, she or he will have access to your Google Classroom as a teacher. Any teacher that you add can do everything in the classroom that you can, except for deleting the class. This function is useful in many scenarios:

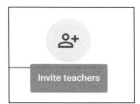

- When you have a co-teacher of your class

- When you want to include special education teachers in your classroom

- When you want to include specialists (reading, math, etc.) in your classroom

- When you want to include instructional coaches or administrators in your classroom

- When you have a student teacher in your classroom

- When you have a long-term substitute

Once an invitation is issued and the co-teacher accepts the role, they will have access to any student information that you can see. Make sure to only invite those who should have access. You can remove co-teachers from the classroom at any time.

Invite teachers

Type a name or email

Teachers you add can do everything you can, except delete the class.

Cancel   Invite

The next section on the page is labeled "Students." You'll see text reading, "Invite students or give them the class code," followed by the unique class code you were automatically assigned when you created the class.

Students can gain entrance to a class in one of two ways. Invite students to join the classroom via email or direct them verbally to classroom.google.com and give them the class code. First, let's discuss how to invite students to your class via email.

Inviting Students to Classroom via Email

By clicking the Invite icon to the left of the Students heading, you will initiate a pop-up window. If you are using Google Classroom in conjunction with your school GFE program, your students' emails should be preloaded. Simply type in their names and you will be able to click on the correct email addresses. If your students are not preloaded into your contacts, you will have to type in email addresses individually. It is important to remember that you may only invite people to your class who share your school domain or who are from a trusted domain (see your GFE administrator to find out if your school has any trusted domain partners). Your school's domain name is how Google recognizes you and the other members of your organization. For example, if your school email address is teacher@sampleschool.com, your domain is sampleschool.com, and all of your students must share that domain name in order to be admitted to your Google Classroom.

For the most part, this system provides excellent access for students and privacy for your online learning community. However, it can sometimes be problematic. If you work for a special education cooperative that services several school districts, for example, you may interact with students with email addresses from varying domains. Some school districts even assign separate domains 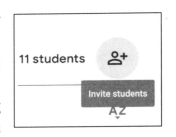 for teachers and students. If this is an issue for you, contact your district's Google for Education administrator about whitelisting trusted domains. Whitelisting enables people in different domains to interact using G Suite for Education, but can only be initiated through the GFE administrator console.

From the window, choose the students you wish to invite. You can do this by scrolling through the list of contacts or by typing the student's name or email address in the search bar. When you see the name of the student you'd like to add, simply click the box to the left of that name to check it. Once the name is checked, it will be added to a list at the bottom of the window. Once you've checked all the students you'd like to invite, click the Invite button. This will send a mass invitation to all the students you've selected to join your Google Classroom.

If you have emailing groups set up, you can also type in the group email and click the Invite button, and an email will be sent to each member of the group, asking them to join your Google Classroom.

The email sent to students will provide them with your name, the class title, and a clickable link that will lead them directly to your Google Classroom.

Once you have invited students, their names will appear on a list under the Students tab. If a student has not yet accepted the invitation to join, the name will be grayed out but an Invited notation will appear to its left. Once she or he accepts the invitation, their name will no longer be grayed out, and you will have successfully added them to your Google Classroom.

Using the Class Code to Join a Class

Your other option is to share the unique class code with your students. You could email it to them or write it on your board the first day of class. In order to join the class using the class code, students will first have to go to classroom.google.com and sign in with their school email address and password.

Note: If a student is having difficulty signing in, it may be because they are already signed in to Google with a personal Gmail address. If that is the case, have them log out and log back in with their school email address. If this does not solve the problem, contact your school's Google for Education administrator, who will be able to pinpoint what's wrong via the administrative console.

After students have successfully signed in to Google Classroom, they must click the plus sign in the top-right corner of the page and choose "Join Class." A pop-up will ask the student to enter the class code. It is case sensitive and should be entered exactly. Once the student enters the class code, they will click the Join button to be taken to the Google Classroom with which the code is associated. They will now be enrolled in the class.

Choosing Student Settings

Back on the People tab, you'll see students beginning to populate your Google Classroom. As they join, the Invited notation will disappear, and they will officially become a student of your classroom. In the Student View of your Google Classroom, the Students tab is labeled "Classmates." When students click on the Classmates tab, they see the names of all their peers enrolled in the class.

For teachers, the People tab is not just for inviting students to the Google Classroom, it is also the key to student management within the app. A drop-down menu labeled Actions is located at the top of the list of students. Checking the box next to the Actions drop-down box above the student names and then clicking in the drop-down menu reveals three actions you can take: Email, Remove, and Mute. The drop-down box will become clickable when you check the box next to it or when you click the checkbox next to specific students. This allows you to make changes for the whole class or just a single individual.

Actions

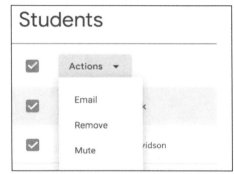

- **Email:** Click the checkbox next to a student name (or multiple names) on your roster and then click the Email button to initiate an email to the student(s).

- **Remove:** Click the checkbox next to a student name (or multiple names) on your roster and then click the Remove button. This completely removes the student(s) from the class. Use this when a student has joined your class in error or dropped your class. If you remove students by accident, don't worry. You can always invite them again!

- **Mute:** Click the checkbox next to a student name (or multiple names) on your roster and then click the Mute button to eliminate a particular student's ability to post and comment. If you have a problem with only a few students making inappropriate comments, you may consider using this option rather than eliminating commenting and/or posting for the entire class.

You will also see an "Invite guardians" option next to each student. Clicking "Invite guardians" initiates a pop-up box requesting the email address of the student's parent or guardian. Once you're done typing the email address, simply click Invite and the guardian will receive an email summary of their child's work, including missing assignments, upcoming work, and class announcements. If you have multiple classrooms with the same student, you can initiate parent summaries for each class.

If you do not see the "Invite guardians" option, it could be because your administrator has not turned this on in the administrative console. Request your local administrator to enable this feature. Once you invite guardians, each will receive an email invitation to accept the summaries and be able to choose how they would like to receive summaries. Guardians can choose to receive weekly or daily email summaries, and they can unsubscribe at any time. If no work is posted that week or if there is no student activity, a summary will not be emailed.

Clicking the three dots icon next to any students' names will give you four options: "Email student," "Email guardians," "Invite guardians," or "Remove guardians." These are self-explanatory.

Now that you know how to add and manage students in your Google Classroom, it's time to start adding content.

The Stream

Click Stream in your top menu bar to go to your stream. Like your Twitter or Facebook feed, the stream is the feed for your classroom that lists all the assignments and posts, with the most recent post showing up first. You will have to scroll down the stream to access any earlier postings.

Post an Announcement

The main body of the Stream page displays two sections. The first features your profile picture and says "Share something with your class…" If you click in this box, it will initiate a text box that you can fill in. However, note that there is a Reuse Post icon (two arrows facing opposite directions) on the right side of the box. Clicking this will allow you to choose any post from this class or another to use again, saving you from having to type the same announcement more than once.

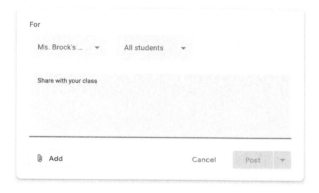

Once you click to type in the announcement box, an announcement window will appear. By default, anything you post here will be shared with all the students in the class you are working in. Whenever you add an announcement, you'll see a drop-down menu that shows the name of the classroom in which you are posting. Clicking this menu brings up a checklist of all the classes you've created in Google Classroom. If you have multiple classes, you can choose to cross post your announcement. To post in more than one of your classes, simply add a check mark next to each of the classrooms in which you'd like the message to appear. This function will save you from having to enter the same announcement multiple times.

Posting an announcement is easy. Simply start typing in the "Share with your class" text box. Before you start announcing news to your students, let's learn about the announcement's purpose, posting instructions, and potential uses.

Announcements can be messages, videos, web pages, or other pieces of content that you send out to your students. Unlike an assignment, students can only look at an announcement, rather than respond with some sort of work. Below each posted announcement, there is a space for you and your students (depending on the student permissions you've established) to add comments, however.

Adding Announcements

You have several options for creating an announcement. You may just want to post a text-only message, such as the one in the photo below. In this example, a teacher has posted a text-only announcement to remind students to turn in permission slips for an upcoming field trip.

Alternatively, you may want to deliver some sort of material using the announcement attachment tools. There are four different options for attaching content to an announcement. You can add files from Google Drive, add a link from the web, add a file uploaded from your device, or link a YouTube video.

Attaching Google Drive Files. Clicking the Google Drive icon brings up a window that shows the files in your Google Drive. There is a menu at the top of the page that includes: Recent, Upload, My Drive, Shared Drives, Starred. These are just different areas in which files are saved within your Google Drive. Typically, using  the search bar just below the menu items is the quickest way to find the document you are looking for. Once you've located the Drive file you want to attach, simply click it to highlight it and click Add at the bottom of the window. It will automatically attach to your announcement.

Adding Web Links. The next option for attaching content to an announcement is by adding a link. Clicking "Add link" will initiate a window in which you can type or paste the URL of the page you'd like your students to visit. You might want them to check out a site to review concepts or read an article. Remember, if you want a due date attached to whatever you're posting, you'll need to use the Assignment function. If it's simply information you want students to consume, however, you can post it as an announcement.

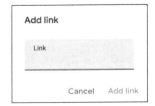

Uploading Computer Files. Clicking the paper clip icon brings up a window that allows you to attach files from your computer. It's the same window that opens when you click to add Drive files, but this defaults to the Upload menu option. Simply drag the files you'd like to upload into the window or click "Select files from your computer" to choose files from your hard drive, external drive, flash drive, etc., to upload to your Google Classroom.

Adding YouTube Videos. The YouTube icon allows you to link to a video from YouTube to add to your stream. Clicking the icon produces a window that allows you two options:

> **Video Search.** You can search YouTube directly from this tab by using keywords. For example, if you were teaching students how to solve quadratic equations by factoring and wanted them to watch a few examples of the process before your lesson, you could use the Video Search function to find appropriate examples by typing in the keywords "quadratic equations factoring." Search results will always be listed in order of popularity based on your keywords, just as they are when searching directly on the YouTube site. Be sure to watch a video in its entirety before posting it to your Google Classroom to ensure that it is appropriate for your students and relevant to your purpose.

> **URL.** If you already know which video you'd like to post and do not need to use the search function, simply click on the URL tab and paste in the video's web address.

After using either method to select a video, click the Add button.

Once you've added the relevant content—you can add multiple files from different sources—prepare a message to go along with the video and click Post to share it with the class. It will appear as an announcement on your stream.

Cross-Posting an Announcement

As you are adding announcements to your classroom stream, you should be aware of a few more tools you can use.

Editing, Deleting, and Copying Announcements

The final features of the announcement function appear after you have already posted your message. A column of three dots can be seen in the top-right corner of each posted announcement. Click there to edit or delete the announcement you've created or to copy a unique link that goes to the announcement. Once you've made the necessary edits, click Save to update the post.

The second section of your Google Classroom Stream page will only appear before you start posting assignments. It simply lists features of the stream including creating and scheduling announcements and responding to student posts. Nothing in this box is clickable; it simply tells you the purpose of the stream. It will disappear as soon as you've posted your first announcement or assignment.

Classwork Tab

Clicking the Classwork tab will bring you to the page where you can begin assigning work to students. You can create assignments and questions for your students, you can use topics to keep classwork organized, and you can order work so students see it in a specific sequence. Before you begin creating your first assignment, let's look at some of the features of this page.

Click on the Create button in the top left-hand corner of the screen to create an assignment. (We'll come back to that in a minute.) On the right-hand side of the page you will see links to Google Calendar and Class Drive folder.

Google Calendar

We've already seen the in-app calendar that Google Classroom automatically generates, but Classroom will also create a calendar for each of your classes on Google Calendar as well. Google Calendar is a separate app, but it can help you set reminders and appointments, and includes other productivity tools. If you have a Google account, you have Google Calendar. No need to sign up. It's the same username and login as all your other Google applications.

If you click on Google Calendar, it will take you to this separate application. If you're already a Google Calendar (calendar.google.com) user, you will have noticed that Google automatically has added a calendar for each of the Google Classrooms you teach and are enrolled in as a student. This calendar is automatically populated based on the due dates assigned in Google Classroom. If a time is specified within a due date, the assignment will show up at that particular time in your Google Calendar. If no time is specified, it will show up as an all-day event on the due date.

You can also add custom events like guest speakers or field trips to your individual Classroom calendars. These are automatically added to your students' Google Calendars as well. Just like any other Google Calendar, you may share your Classroom calendar with any other Google user. This includes those outside of your educational organization. You can also make the calendar public or embed it into your teaching website in order to share assignment due dates and upcoming events with parents and other interested parties.

Class Drive Folder

Clicking the "Class Drive folder" will again take you to Google Drive, where all the content you have generated for your Google Classroom will be stored. Each assignment is given its own file folder. From this folder you will see that a subfolder is created for each assignment where you can access student work. You can also access all your templates that you create for use in your Google Classroom. Remember, never delete this folder. It's the filing cabinet for everything you and your students do in your Google Classroom!

Creating Classwork

The Create button on the Classwork page is, as they say, where the magic happens. The most significant benefits of Google Classroom are right here, with this function. Once teachers initiate the assignment flow process, it can be done from start to finish, completely paperless. The "assignment flow process" refers to the various stages in the life of an assignment. Broken down into steps, assignment flow looks like this:

    1. Teacher creates assignment.

    2. Student opens and completes assignment.

    3. Student turns in assignment.

    4. Teacher grades assignment and returns with comments.

    5. Repeat as necessary.

With Google Classroom, teachers can remain in constant contact with the student throughout the entire workflow process.

As noted, Google Classroom works most effectively when combined with the other Google for Education apps. Consider having students write assignments in Google Docs and create presentations in Google Slides instead of using Word or PowerPoint. Utilizing these programs allows you to look in on the progress of student papers and projects and offer feedback before the final due date.

Typically, teachers create an assignment and don't see it again until it is turned in for grading. Using G Suite for Education, both teachers and students can have access to assignments from the very beginning. As a teacher, you can access a document remotely while the student is working and make suggestions and offer feedback in real time. This is far more relevant than a few red-ink comments given weeks after an assignment has been turned in.

Not all of your assignments will be created using Google Docs or other Google for Education apps, but incorporating those programs into the Google Classroom process will significantly increase its functionality and usefulness.

Creating an Assignment

So how do you create an assignment? In the Classwork tab, clicking the Create button with the plus icon will open an assignment window. The first step is to decide what kind of assignment you want to create. Google Classroom offers five options:

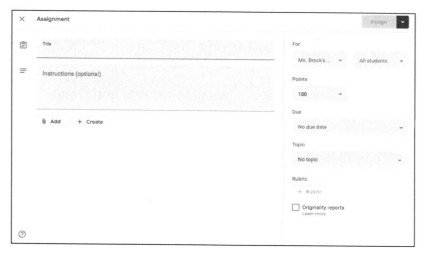

- Assignment

- Quiz assignment

- Question

- Material

- Reuse post

Below those, there is also an item that reads "Topics." We'll talk more about that on page 45. In this section we'll go over what each of these five options offer so you can choose the exact right assignment for the work you have in mind.

Let's begin by creating a basic assignment. Click Assignment on the list. This will take you to a new window where you can begin to build your assignment.

First, you will be asked to give your assignment a title. Creating a consistent and logical naming scheme is strongly encouraged because for every assignment created in Google

Classroom, a folder of the same name is created in Google Drive. The students' finished assignments are kept in these folders. If there is a discrepancy with a grade or whether or not something was turned in, or if you simply want to access a past assignment for assessment purposes, you'll want to be able to locate it quickly and easily.

Alice Keeler, who provides Google Classroom tips and tricks on her website, AliceKeeler .com, recommends using a numerical system (i.e., Biology.001 or #001 Biology). You may also consider organizing by unit and type of assignment (i.e., Assignment 1.1 would be the first assignment in Unit 1, and Quiz 2.3 is the third quiz in Unit 2). No matter what naming convention you concoct, it should be easy to remember for both you and your students in order to retrieve assignments as efficiently as possible.

Each student also has an automatically created Google Classroom file in his or her Google Drive folder. Each time you create an assignment, a folder of the same name will appear in their file as well. In this way, each student will have a record of the work they have done throughout the year. This intuitive filing system can prove invaluable when it comes to evaluation and assessment of learning outcomes.

Now that you've named your assignment, we're going to add all the relevant details. Your next task is to add instructions. This is optional, but well worth your time to prevent having to answer questions from students about the directions over and over. In this area, you can include the instructions, expectations, goals, etc., of the assignment. If you have a rubric, you may want to include that as an attachment since assignment posts can have multiple attachments.

Under the instructions section, you'll find two options: Add and Create.

Adding Assignments

Adding content to an assignment works in the same way as adding content to announcements. Simply click the Add button. From there you can add Google Drive content, links, uploaded files, or YouTube videos.

Creating Assignments

If you click the Create button, you can create assignment content from scratch using a variety of Google apps, including Docs, Slides, Sheets, Drawings, and Forms. Clicking on any one of those will create a blank file to which you can add your content. Once you've completed your document or relevant addition, click the Share button in the top-right corner. This will open a window that shows you will be sharing the content to your Google Classroom and that you are the owner of the file. You can type in the names or email addresses of any other relevant people that you'd like to share this document with. When you are finished, click Done and close out of the window. You will now see that the attachment has been added to the assignment.

Add all the content that is necessary to completing the assignment. Remember that you may attach more than one piece of content. For example, in a single assignment post, a teacher might upload a rubric from his or her computer, add a Google Slides template for a presentation, and include a link to a website that explains how to correctly cite academic sources. Attach as much as you think is necessary for your students to successfully get the job done.

Editing Permissions

Next you will adjust the viewing and editing permissions on any Google Drive document you've attached to the assignment. Let's imagine you want students to fill out a short questionnaire you've created in Google Docs as an introductory activity for the beginning of the year. In a drop-down menu next to the Google Docs file you have attached, you'll find three options: "Students can view file," "Students can edit file," and "Make a copy for each student."

Students can view file. Choosing this option allows students to open the document but not change it in any way. In other words, they can look but not touch.

Students can edit file. This allows students to add to, change, and delete content on the document you've attached. This option is helpful if you are conducting a group brainstorming activity or selecting time slots for presentations. All students can make their mark on a single shared document.

Make a copy for each student. This final option is most appropriate for the sample activity above. When you indicate the "Make a copy for each student" option, Google will generate a unique document for each student using his or her name when the student opens the file. So the file you've named "Assignment.001—Student Introduction" when opened by your student Lila Smith will become "Assignment.001—Student Introduction—Lila Smith." And so on for each student in the class.

This is an excellent option to use when you are providing a document or worksheet to be filled out by the students. It's kind of like a virtual copy machine!

You do not have to create or add anything to go with the assignment. You may simply provide the instructions to the assignment, and the students will create their own documents, presentations, or projects from directly in Google Classroom or upload their work at a later time.

Assignment Details

Assigning the Work to Specific Students and Classes

To the left of the assignment panel, you will see a section that asks you to enter relevant details about the assignment. The first section—For—will allow you to choose all the classes in which you want to post this assignment. There is also a section that allows you to choose specific students who will receive the assignment. This defaults to assigning all students the assignment, but if you have specialized group projects or activities that include a single student or small groups of students, you can specify here who will receive the assignment.

Assigning Point Value

Next you choose the amount of points the assignment will be worth. The default is 100 points, but you can change this to any number. Clicking in the point area will also allow you to make the assignment "ungraded," which means no point value will be attached to it.

Assigning a Due Date

Next, you are asked to provide a due date for the assignment. This date is important because it will be included in reminders to students and used in organizing the Upcoming

Assignments widget next to both student and teacher streams, as well as in the in-app calendar and the Google Calendar. You may also add a specific time that the assignment is due; otherwise, the assignment will be considered late if it is not turned in by 11:59 p.m. of the due date indicated.

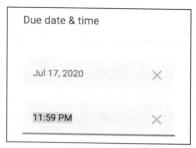

You also have the option to include no due date at all. You may use this feature when providing optional extra credit opportunities, or in any other scenario in which a due date is unnecessary. Simply leave it with "No due date."

Adding a Topic

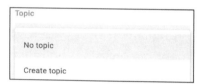

The next section is for Topic. Topics are a relatively new addition to Google Classroom and are very useful for organizing assignments. If you click in the Topic area, you will see all the topics you have created. If you haven't created any yet, you may choose from "No topic" or "Create topic." Please note that if you do not choose a topic for your assignment, it cannot be reordered unless it falls under a topic.

Some ideas for topics include:

- Subjects (math, reading, science, etc.)

- Units (Revolutionary War, Civil War, etc.)

- Types of work (daily work, essays, exams, etc.)

Once you decide on the types of topics you want to use to organize your classroom, click "Create topic." As you create new topics, you will be able to choose from them as they will be saved and populate the topics list in the drop-down in this area of each assignment.

Adding a Rubric

Next, you will see an area to attach a rubric to any assignment. This is a feature currently being beta tested, but it may become a permanent part of Google Classroom when it is out of this phase. If the Rubric button is grayed out, you cannot use it unless your administrator turns on the beta-testing feature (as of June 2020). If you do have access to create and attach rubrics to your assignment, simply click the Add Rubric button and choose whether you want to create a rubric, reuse a rubric you have already created, or import a rubric from Google Sheets.

For our purposes, we'll go over creating a rubric in case it is an option to you. Know that any rubric you create can be reused for other assignments. To create a rubric, simply click "Create rubric." This will take you to a Rubric Creation window where you will outline your criteria, the levels within each criterion, and the associated point value. You may add up to fifty criteria in a rubric.

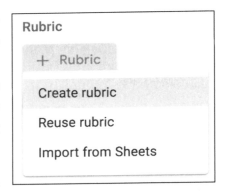

In the sample below, the teacher is adding a criterion for organization of a paper. The title is "Organization," and the description explains how to meet the criteria. The teacher then creates "levels" of each criterion, in this case: Exceeds Expectations, Meets Expectations, Partially Meets Expectations, and "Does not meet expectations." Each level is given a title, point value, and description. For example, if there are ten possible points in the criterion, the highest level, Exceeds Expectations, would be worth ten points. Each descending level would have a lower point value. You can use these rubrics to easily grade different features of student work. To add levels, simply click the plus sign. To add a criterion, click the "Add a criterion" button at the bottom. Once you are finished, click Save, and the rubric will be attached to the assignment for use in grading and for student use.

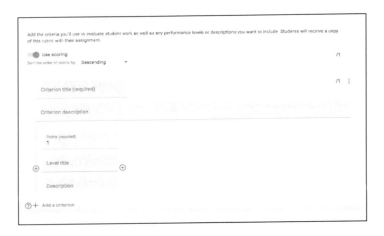

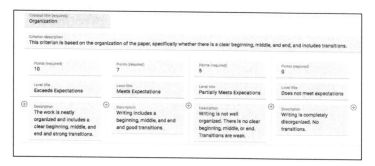

Originality Reports

Originality reporting is also a newer function in Google Classroom. In the free version of Google Classroom, teachers can only use this function three times in a class. The originality report will detect plagiarism in student work. Save the use of this feature for big assignments like papers and exams. Remember, you can only use it three times unless your GFE administrator upgrades your school Google account.

Once you've completed all the relevant information, you can assign the work! Do this by clicking the Assign button in the top-right corner of the screen. Note there is a drop-down menu where you can choose to Assign, Schedule (denote a specific date when you want the assignment to go live), or "Save draft" (if you don't have time to finish it). You can also discard the draft if you want to start again.

Whew! It seems like creating an assignment is a lot of work, but once you get used to the process it goes very quickly! Remember, you don't have to use all these features, but they are available if you need them.

Publishing an Assignment

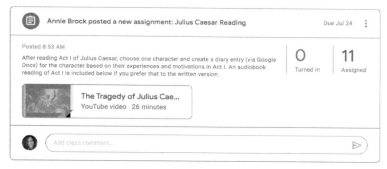

After you publish an assignment, it will appear in the classroom stream much like an announcement, but with a few differences. You'll have the option to make comments on assignments, as will students if you've elected to give them that permission. But you'll also see the addition of some key information. Looking at an assignment in the stream in Teacher View, you will see the due date and time for the assignment (in the example on page 47, the due date is July 24), as well as a running count of how many students in the class have turned in the assignment.

When clicked, the three vertical dots icon next to the due date brings up a menu of options: "Move to top," Edit, and Delete.

Move to top. Clicking this option bumps a post to the top of the class stream. You might use this function to help students easily locate an announcement posted far in the past that has been buried under new items. If you notice that several students have yet to turn in an upcoming project, you can move that assignment to the top of the stream as a reminder for students to keep on top of it, so to speak.

Edit. This option allows you to make changes and corrections to a post.

Delete. This option removes a post completely from your stream. If you delete an assignment, any associated attachments will remain in the Google Drive folder.

Assignments in Student View

Students viewing an assignment in their own streams have an area to add comments to the post, assuming you have given them that permission. Clicking on the title of the assignment takes students to a page that includes any instructions and/or attachments you've provided. In addition, it will allow them to see any comments or discussions that have been posted on the assignment. This is also where they will turn in work and mark it as done.

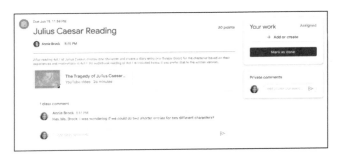

Introduction to **Google Classroom**

To the right of the assignment's details, there is a box titled "Your work." In this area, students will know whether or not the assignment is past due by the presence of the red Missing text in the upper-right corner. Google Classroom generates this warning when students fail to mark assignments as done before the due date indicated.

Otherwise, there will be a green Assigned status for work that hasn't been turned in yet, a "Turned in" for work that has been submitted, or a "Turned in late" for work that was submitted after the indicated due date.

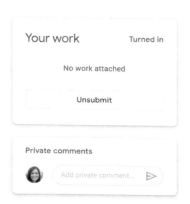
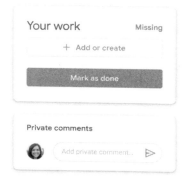
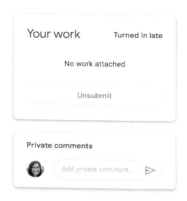

Completing an Assignment

If you ask students to create work for the assignment, they will be able to add it here by clicking the "Add or create" button, which will allow them to attach created files from Google Drive, a web link, or by uploading a file. Students working via the mobile app can also upload material from the camera roll. In addition, they can create something new via Google applications. These include Docs for writing essays and other word processing tasks, Slides for creating presentations, Sheets for developing spreadsheets, and Drawings for rendering diagrams, charts, and other design-based tasks. Any materials created using these tools are

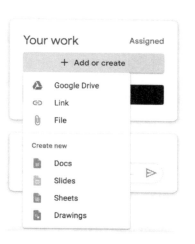

automatically posted on the assignment and shared with the teacher from the moment they are created. This means that if a student fails to click the "Mark as Done" button to indicate they have finished an assignment, a teacher can still go into the student's file to evaluate whatever work has been completed or how much has been done.

Clicking "Create new Doc," for example, will automatically generate a blank document attached to the assignment with the student's name and the title of the assignment. This is great for staying organized and checking in on student assignments as they are working, since all student-created files in Google Classroom are automatically shared with the teacher.

Being Part of the Process

Because all files that students create can be viewed and edited by the teacher, the teacher can access student content from the Assignment screen the moment it is added or created. Students should be encouraged to use this function as soon as they start an assignment, as it allows you to be part of the creation process from the beginning. This gives you an opportunity to access student work and offer guidance and feedback every step of the way.

Turning in an Assignment

It is up to the students to turn in the required work by clicking the "Mark as done" button to indicate they have completed the assignment. Once this button is clicked and the assignment is turned in, the assignment can still be unsubmitted by the student to make changes. However, if the assignment is resubmitted after the due date, it will be marked as late even if the student initially submitted the assignment before the due date.

Mark as done

Either way, once something has been uploaded or attached to the assignment by the student, the "Mark as done" button changes to a "Turn in" button. The distinction between the two is that "Mark as done" indicates that a student has completed an assignment task, but it did not require them to upload or attach any digital content (i.e., "Read chapter two" or "Construct a suspension bridge model using cardboard and string"). The "Turn in" button indicates that the student is going to turn in a piece of digital content as part of the assignment.

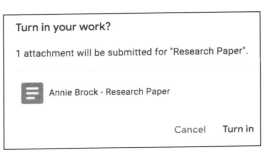

Turn in your work?

1 attachment will be submitted for "Research Paper".

Annie Brock - Research Paper

Cancel   Turn in

Once a student clicks the "Turn in" button, they will be greeted with a window asking them if they are sure they'd like to submit the work. This second-chance screen gives students the opportunity to change their minds before they turn in the assignment. Once a student confirms they would like to submit the assignment, the assignment page changes to include an Unsubmit option.

Unsubmitting an Assignment

In Student View, students can unsubmit previously turned in work to make changes. Again, if the work is unsubmitted prior to the due date and subsequently resubmitted after the due date, the student's work will be considered late by the system. A student will know whether or not a finished assignment was turned in late by the presence of an indicator in the top-right corner of the Assignment page. These clear time stamps and late indicators can alleviate many classroom issues, since they make it nearly impossible for teachers to lose track of submitted assignments or for students to engage in deceptive practices.

On both the Teacher and Student view of an assignment page, there is a box labeled "Add private comment." This can serve as a quick messaging system between students and teachers to ask questions about the assignment or to give feedback. You will be notified when a private comment is posted from a student and vice versa.

Other Types of Assignments

Now that you've mastered creating an assignment, let's go over other types of assignments you can also give to your students. Remember, when you hit the Create button in the Classwork tab, you are presented with a range of options. We'll go through each of those now.

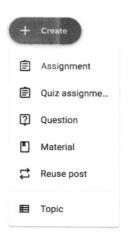

Quiz Assignment

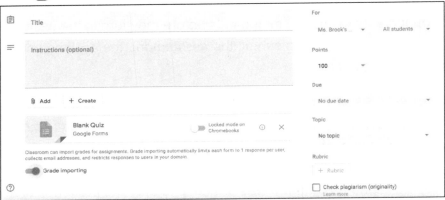

Selecting "Quiz assignment" will generate an assignment page identical to the regular assignment page with one big difference: it generates a blank Google Form quiz for you to fill out. To create the quiz, click the Google Form icon. This will take you to the blank quiz. Here you can title the quiz and add a variety of questions, including multiple choice, essay, short answers, etc. You can also assign a point value to each question in the quiz and include an answer key if you want the quiz to be automatically graded. When you are finished creating the quiz, simply close the window. Everything in Google apps is saved in real time, so you don't have to worry about losing your work. The quiz will be attached to your assignment. If your students have Chromebooks, you can use the toggle to make sure the quiz is taken in locked mode (this means the students will not be able to open other tabs or applications while taking the quiz). Once you've finished entering in the rest of the assignment details (just like before!), click Assign to post the quiz to the classroom stream.

Question

Question is the next option for creating an assignment. This allows you to pose a question to the entire class for students to answer. Posting a question assignment to the classroom stream is a great way to start a discussion, take a poll, or conduct a quick formative assessment. You can use this feature to spark question-driven discussions or do a quick check for understanding in order to help engage students. In the example shown in the figure above, a teacher is checking for existing knowledge before starting a unit on World War II.

The Question feature is very similar to the Assignment feature. When creating a question post, you can attach supplementary computer documents, Google Drive files, YouTube videos, and web links. Simply type in the question you'd like to ask and add any pertinent details and additional materials. Questions, like assignments, are accompanied by due dates and can be graded in the exact same manner. Once your details are sorted and you're ready to ask the question, just click Ask. You can also save a draft of a question just like you can save assignment drafts.

On the student side, once they answer a question, they can also peruse and comment on their classmates' answers. You will be able to see the turned-in answers from your Grading dashboard, which we will discuss on page 56.

Material

The next assignment option is Material. This is simply to provide material to the students. You can assign material posts to students, multiple classes, and topics, but they are not graded. They are simply a way to upload or link content for student use.

Reuse Post

This is the same as reusing an announcement. Clicking "Reuse post" will bring up a list of your classes. Choose the class that has the assignment you want to reuse, choose that assignment, and then change any relevant details for the new assignment. Then post as normal.

Topic

The final area of the Create function is Topic. Again, it's a good idea to create topics because then you can reorder posts easily by dragging and dropping within the topic. Topics might include units of study, subjects, or types of work. Creating topics takes a little more work up front, but it will be worth it when you are easily reorganizing your assignments in the stream later on.

The Assignment Page

Each assignment is given its own assignment page. You can easily go to the assignment page by clicking on a created assignment in the stream.

First, notice the menu bar at the top of the page. In its center are two tabs: Instructions and "Student work."

The Instructions tab displays information about the assignment, including its title and the details you provided when you initially posted it. The due date, class comments, and any attachments are also displayed. This view shows you essentially all the information available to students through the class stream.

The "Student work" tab is more complex and so will need further elaboration.

Student Work

The "Student work" tab includes information only you can see. Its menu, which appears immediately below the assignment page menu, provides a Return button to give the graded assignment back to students and a drop-down menu to assign it a point value.

Downloading Student Grades

At the far right of the "Student work" menu bar is a gear icon that, when clicked, offers you the opportunity to copy all grades to Google Sheets, download all grades as CSV, or download these grades as CSV ("these grades" refers to the grades on this specific assignment). All data will be downloaded as a .csv file that you can use to transfer grades from Google Classroom to your electronic grade book, where compatible. (CSV stands for "comma-separated values"—it's a universal format for moving data between applications such as spreadsheets.)

Viewing the Roster

In the left sidebar of this page, there is a roster of students enrolled in the class. The roster is divided into two sections: "Turned in" and Assigned. This area is where you will indicate the grade each student receives on the assignment and write private comments for students about their work. Clicking the name of a student on the roster causes the main area of the screen to show details of that particular student's assignment, including any attachments.

Choosing Assignment Icons

Below the menus, the name of the assignment appears at the top of the page in large, bold text. You will also note large numbers indicating how many students have turned in the assignment and how many have not. Below this are rows of square icons, one for each student enrolled in the class, which also indicate whether the assignment has been completed or remains unfinished. These icons, in addition to the running tally at the top of the web page, show teachers visually whether or not students have submitted their work. For example, the assignment page example shows that one of the students in the class has turned in the assignment.

Clicking the arrow next to the All button displays a drop-down menu to allow the teacher to view icons for specific students, including those who have turned in the assignment, those who have not, and those whose assignments have been graded.

Displaying Individual Assignments

To view a specific student's work, click either the student's name in the left sidebar or the student's icon in the main area of the screen. To evaluate an assignment, click on the student's attachment(s), and it will automatically open in a new browser tab. Once you've looked over the work, simply close that tab to automatically return to your Google Classroom tab. If the assignment was created with a Google application, there is no need to worry about saving as you add comments. Google apps automatically save after every keystroke, so your comments will not be lost even if your computer crashes.

Grading Assignments

At this point, you'll be ready to grade the assignment. In the Points drop-down list in the Student Work menu, you can indicate the point value an assignment is worth. You will indicate the point value here (if it has changed from your original indication) or you can change the point value to "ungraded."

Once a point value is assigned, you can enter student grades. Click on the blank space next to a student's name on the roster in the left-hand sidebar. In the example pictured, the student earned 18 points out of 20. Here you also have the opportunity to offer feedback by way of adding a private comment. Simply type the feedback in the "Add private comment…" box and click Post. Once you have posted a private comment, you can click on the three dots to its right side to edit or delete it.

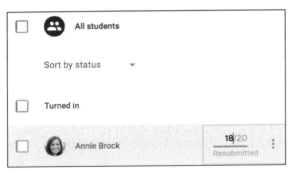

Viewing Submission Histories

An additional feature on the student's assignment page is the ability to view the student's submission history for this assignment. Click "See history" under the student's name at the top of the page. This allows you to see when the student submitted and/or unsubmitted the assignment, and how many times this was done before the due date.

Return work to 1 student?

Student will be notified and can check any grade you've left.

Annie Brock 18/20

Private comment

Cancel Return

Returning Assignments

When you're done with grading and commenting, simply click the Return button at the top left of the screen (or choose Return by clicking the three dots next to the grade) to give back students their graded work. Any students with a check mark next to their names will receive their grades and comments. In order to do a bulk return so that all students receive their graded assignments simultaneously, wait until you have graded every student's work and then click all the blank boxes to fill them with check marks. All selected students will have their work returned to them.

After returning student work, a pop-up window will remind you that each student will automatically receive an email indicating that you have graded the assignment. They will be allowed to view their scores and your comments at this time.

Changing Grades

Classroom allows you to change the grade of assignments after your original assessment.

This is a fantastic feature, particularly if the student needs another opportunity to successfully complete the assignment and demonstrate mastery. The process is exactly the same as it is for first entering a grade, and you even have the chance to add new comments. Simply click Return when you've made the necessary changes. Students will be alerted to any changes in their assignment grades via email.

The Classroom Workflow Advantage

There you have it. This process of assigning, grading, and returning is known as the assignment flow. It may seem like a time-consuming process, but once you learn the steps it goes very quickly, especially when you consider all the tasks that the assignment flow is replacing.

Before digital tools like Google Classroom, you would go to the copy machine to make copies of the assignment for each student. Then, you would pass out the copies, dictate instructions, and answer any student questions. The students would then take the assignment home, and, if it wasn't misplaced or otherwise forgotten, they would finish it and physically hand it in on the due date. After students handed in the assignment, you would collect the papers, take them home, grade them, record the grades in the grade book, take the assignments back to school, and deliver them to each student with handwritten comments and feedback.

Google Classroom removes almost all the potential for error and frustration in the assignment flow. Assignments are stored in the virtual world, not to be lost in the cluttered bottom of a backpack. Reminders are consistently sent and displayed so that students are always aware of due dates, and teachers receive clear notifications when those due dates are not met. Teachers no longer have to spend time fixing paper jams in the copy machine or lugging home workbooks to be graded by hand.

In addition to solving many of the missteps that can happen in the process of assigning student work, Google Classroom also offers many opportunities for communication and clarification on assignments. Not to mention, utilizing Google Classroom creates a digital record of the work a student has completed through-out the year, helping schools assess and evaluate long-term student progress.

The best feature of Google Classroom's assignment flow, however, is that a teacher can pop in at any point in the process to offer guidance and feedback. The lines of communication are open from the time the assignment is initiated to the moment it is turned in—and beyond!

Grading Questions and Quizzes

As already stated, questions are graded in the same way as assignments. Assign a point value (or choose Ungraded), grade the student's answer, and then return the work. Just like you can comment on assignments, you can add comments to returned student answers. If you have included an answer key for the quizzes, they will be automatically graded, and the students can view their grades as soon as the quiz has been finished.

Grades

The Grades tab is the final menu item at the top of the computer screen. This is essentially an online gradebook. It keeps track of student points on each assignment, plus a running overall grade for each student, as well as a class average on each assignment. This is very similar to PowerSchool and other comparable applications. Using the Grades tab gives you an overview of everything students are missing, their overall grade, and how well they've performed on assignments they've submitted.

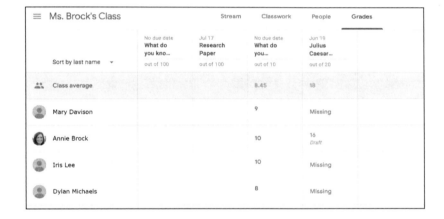

Part 3

Tips and Recommendations for Classroom Users

As you read this step-by-step guide for operating Google Classroom, remember that Google is adding features all the time, some of which may not be addressed here. If you're unfamiliar with a new feature, just play around with it! It's important to remember that everything you do in Classroom can be undone. If you post something by mistake, you can delete it. If you delete something by mistake, you can retrieve it. Trial and error is key to becoming an experienced Classroom user.

Here are a few final tips and recommendations for using Google Classroom:

- Download and use the Chrome browser to get access to apps and add-ons that can optimize your G Suite for Education experience.

- Though images in this guide are from the desktop version of Classroom, there are also app-based versions for tablets and smartphones available in the Google Play and Apple App stores. They look very similar to what you've seen here.

- Classroom is available in forty-four languages. Google Apps should default to the language specified in the user's account. Make changes as necessary.

- Follow the students' lead. Sometimes kids can be quicker with technology than grown-ups. Encourage your students to discover different ways to use Classroom, and then put their ideas into practice.

- Ask for help! If you are struggling in some area of Google Classroom, seek advice from other users. Whether your appeal is made to your GFE administrator, a fellow educator, or directly to Google forums or staff via the question mark icon, there will be someone who has faced your particular issue and can help you determine the next steps.

Practical Applications of Google Classroom

Now that you're familiar with the various features and functions of Google Classroom, how can you make the most of it? Once you've created a classroom for your students, it's important to update it regularly, in order to encourage students to check it each day. The more you use Classroom, the easier it will be to operate its various features and pick up on the new ones constantly being released. In this section, you'll find tips and tricks for maximizing the benefits of Google Classroom, as well as ideas for classroom applications.

Professional Development. Google Classroom is an excellent tool for all sorts of learning, including professional development for teachers. Digital professional development is gaining popularity as teachers are able to interact with a professional network and learn new skills and concepts when it's convenient for them. Encourage teachers in your district to create Google Classrooms to share their expertise and insights. One teacher might create a classroom with modules teaching an effective behavioral management plan. Another might create a classroom to demonstrate a new instructional method. These "teach the teacher" opportunities are endless with Google Classroom. An added bonus? Teachers are able to see Google Classroom through the students' lens. Because there are two different interfaces for teacher and student, it's imperative the teacher becomes familiar with what students are seeing.

Online Distance Learning. During the 2019–2020 school year, the coronavirus pandemic forced most schools in the US to close their physical buildings. Many schools moved to online learning, and Google Classroom became a commonly used tool to stay connected to students. Google Classroom is a great way to send assignments and maintain a connection, even when we unexpectedly have to be separated from our students.

Teaming. Google Classroom can also serve as a long-term communication tool for teaming. Teachers in a particular grade, team, group, or committee might use the Classroom tools to conduct conversations on tier groups, specific student needs, or curriculum. The Assignment function can be used when teachers need to turn in a report or submit a lesson plan; the Question function can be used to initiate a conversation on curriculum or student needs; and the Announcement feature can be used to share resources, plan field trips, and coordinate events. The communication options, privacy considerations, and built-in reminders make Classroom an optimal tool for use in teacher groups.

Curriculum Improvement. Gaps and redundancies can exist in even the most well-developed curriculum plans. Consider utilizing Google Classroom as a way to identify and mitigate these issues. For example, a teacher may notice that students are not yet proficient in a skill they should have mastered the year before, and thus present evidence from student work in Google Classroom to the curriculum director to help close the gap. Or it may come to the attention of an administrator, who has joined classrooms in an observatory role, that two teachers are covering the same novel. Identifying and sharing this kind of critical information gleaned from Google Classroom, along with student work as evidence of the knowledge or skills gap, can help shore up any weak areas of the curriculum.

Observation Station. Ask a teacher in your discipline to add you to their Google Classroom so you can see what kinds of things are happening in another class. The act of observing a teacher as she or he interacts with students can be an invaluable learning tool. This could be especially helpful in a mentoring relationship, so that a first-year or student teacher could observe a veteran teacher in action.

Up Your Evaluation Game. Google Classroom can be an extremely useful tool for administrators. Though it would be nice to spend lots of time sitting in on classes and observing teachers and students, that's not always possible. Joining the Google Classrooms of teaching staff as a student can allow an administrator to get a sense of what's happening in any class at any time. This bird's-eye view can also help administrators make better-informed evaluations. An administrator may even pinpoint examples of particularly innovative or effective lessons or projects, and ask teachers to present at a professional development event or otherwise share those tips and techniques with fellow teachers. Used appropriately and responsibly, this type of connectedness has the potential to improve the entire culture of a school.

Bell Ringers. Use the "Ask a question" function to pose a question to the students at the beginning of class time, or post a link to a food-for-thought article or video and ask a question about it. Using the "due date" function, you can make these questions due in the first ten minutes of class so that students will know to get to work on them right away. If students have time after they post an answer, they could comment on other students' answers. This type of open-ended discussion can be a great way to initiate student engagement early in the lesson.

Clubs and Student Groups. Teachers and school personnel can use Google Classroom to share information and coordinate with students in clubs and athletic teams. A football coach could use it to post game film for student athletes to review, or post diagrams for them to study before a big game. A chess club instructor could share a link to an article on strategy or an online chess game. The possibilities are endless! If you have a need to share and communicate with students, you can put Google Classroom to work for you.

Student Portfolios. Anything students create in Google Classroom is kept in a folder on their Google Drive, which means they are keeping a running record of everything they've done throughout the year. A student using Google Classroom essentially has a built-in portfolio of all their work. Using these "portfolios," teachers can have students select their best work to send home or showcase, share work with other education professionals, or evaluate progress students have made over the course of the term.

Photo Documentation. Teachers often assign projects that are not digitally driven, but even then, Google Classroom can be used to virtually showcase that work. An art teacher might instruct students to photograph sculptures they are creating and upload those images to be displayed, commented on, or used for instructional purposes. An English teacher might ask students to hand draw a map of a novel's setting or sketch a character, and then photograph or scan and upload these images so that they become part of their students' digital portfolios. Lessons involving manipulatives and hands-on activities do not necessarily negate the need for Google Classroom. It's still a great way to display work and get feedback.

Get the "Share to Classroom" Extension. The "Share to Classroom" Chrome extension allows teachers to automatically share content they find on the web with students. When both a teacher and his or her students have the extension on their devices (which can be added individually or for everyone by a GFE administrator), the teacher can go to any website, click the "Share to Classroom" button, and like magic, the website pops up on all student devices. This extension prevents you from having to painstakingly dictate long, cumbersome URLs to students. It's also very useful if you want to show students something on the fly. Let's say in the middle of a geography lesson, a student asks where the Nile River empties. The teacher can quickly pull up a map online, click the "Share to Classroom" button, and, just like that, all students in the class can see on their devices a map of the Nile emptying into the Mediterranean Sea. To find the extension, go to the Chrome store and search for "Share to Classroom."

Upload Worksheets. Yes, you can still use premade worksheets. Simply scan the worksheet or document you'd like students to fill out and post it to your classroom. Using the Google Drawing tool, for example, students can create text boxes to fill in the blanks or use the shape tools to draw diagrams. This is a great way to save paper!

Get Student Feedback. Encourage students to utilize the comment stream that comes with each announcement and assignment to ask questions and provide feedback. If students are continually asking the same question or don't understand a directive for a particular assignment, this can signify that a change to your directions is necessary. This feedback can help you tweak and revise assignments to avoid problems and confusion in the future.

Year-End Reflection. Reflection is a major buzzword in education, and for good reason. Teachers should review lessons and units often and with a critical eye in order to continue to provide the best learning experiences for their students. At the end of the term, however, it's sometimes difficult to look back over the entirety of a year or semester and consider changes to the overall structure and flow of the class. But with Google Classroom, teachers have a running record of what went on every day of class. In reviewing the stream, teachers have the opportunity to examine what worked and what didn't, and they can make changes to improve the overall impact of the course.

Attach a Google Form. Though this feature has not yet been implemented at the time of publishing this book, Classroom will soon allow teachers to add a Google Form directly to a post (currently you can add only the link to a Google Form). In Google Forms, you can create surveys, quizzes, and tests, and responses are automatically organized in a spreadsheet for easy grading. Using Google Forms is a simple way to conduct formative assessments quickly and easily. To try out Google Forms, go to forms.google.com.

Talk, Talk, Talk! From bulk emailing to direct messaging, interacting with students has never been easier. There is no shortage of opportunities for teachers to leave comments, notes, feedback, and questions for students. What makes Google Classroom stand out among similar online classroom management tools is its emphasis on communication and ease of sharing information. Take advantage of these opportunities to up your communication game and keep your students engaged in classwork outside of designated class times. Gone are the days of tracking down kids in the halls or trying to find a good time to meet with a student to clear up a small issue. The tools embedded in Google Classroom allow you to simply exchange a quick message with a student to clear up a misunderstanding or refocus a student on the task at hand. Not only is Google Classroom simple and seamless, but it also, in relying on short electronic messages between teachers and students, employs a communication strategy with which most students are already very comfortable.

Behavioral Management. Classroom comes equipped with tools to "mute" disruptive students or delete their comments, but the messaging function is a great way to conduct behavioral management before you have to resort to this option. Simply click the message icon to send a quick email to a student asking them to refocus. It's a great way to make discipline immediate and private without having to single out a student in front of the entire class.

Keep Kids Safe. The ability to quickly view and attach YouTube videos from Google Classroom is a concern for some teachers. Along with many immensely helpful and useful videos, there are some that may be deemed inappropriate for the classroom. Work with your school's Google administrator to use the restriction settings to limit the kinds of YouTube videos students can view.

Turn the Tables. Assign a different student each week to provide a thought-provoking article and discussion question for their peers to answer. Incorporating student-led instruction can help students "buy in" to a topic and feel ownership over their own education. Classroom makes it simple to provide opportunities for students to share their individual passions, which is an easy way to personalize the instruction to suit student interests and introduce the class (and the teacher!) to new ideas.

Bump Those Posts. The "Move to top" feature allows a teacher to move an assignment that has been driven down the stream back to the top. For example, if you assign a book project at the beginning of the term to be completed at the end of the term, you might want to bump the assignment post every few weeks to keep it fresh in the students' minds. When it comes to students, there is no such thing as too many reminders!

Give Feedback to Google. If you or your students would like to see new features added to Google Classroom, use the question mark icon to offer up new ideas. Google team members actually read this feedback, and many of the updates and new features that have been added to Classroom since its inception have come directly from user feedback like this.

Whole-Class Activities. Set up a Google Slide template that students can edit, and ask each student to research and create one slide on a given topic. Give the students a twenty-minute deadline for creating their slide and have each student share their slide.

Bam! You have a class-created presentation made in twenty minutes or less. You can also employ this group-work strategy to brainstorming and note taking. Simply open a Google Doc with open editing privileges and have students start contributing!

Keep Current. Since the program's arrival, Google has added features and updates to Classroom on an almost monthly basis. Click the question mark icon and the What's New text to keep on top of these new features. Additionally, there are some wonderful Facebook groups dedicated to discussing all things Classroom. Join one to see how other professionals are using Classroom across the globe. Or you can search #googleclassroom, #GoogleEDU, or #GSuiteEDU on Twitter to connect with other educators using Google for Education.

Flip Your Classroom. A "flipped classroom" is one in which the instructional portion of a lesson is done as homework, and the homework portion of the lesson is done in the classroom. This allows the student to consume a lecture or watch examples outside of class time, in order to prepare for application of the concept during class time. This also allows active work to be done under the guidance of the teacher. For many people, this model just makes sense; students usually have the most questions when they're in the process of solving a problem or writing an essay. Google Classroom makes this process of flipping a cinch, since you can easily upload video lectures and examples for students to watch and read. They can add any comments or questions these materials spark, and you can be prepared to dive into the lesson the next day.

It's for Everyone! Library media specialists, counselors, speech pathologists, gifted coordinators... Any professional in the school setting can establish a Google Classroom. Even if a staff member doesn't work with students on a daily—or even monthly—basis, a Google Classroom is still a great tool to provide information to students and keep in touch with those in the building. A counselor, for example, could set up a classroom and add every student in the school in order to share anti-bullying or digital citizenship modules and resources. A library media specialist could do the same for academic research techniques or library procedure guidelines. If the goal is communicating with kids quickly and effectively, any education professional can make use of Google Classroom.

Save the Trees. It goes without saying: The paperless nature of Google Classroom is among its most attractive features. Any school interested in saving money or environmental resources can do so with Google Classroom. Consider making a contest out of it. Get teachers trained and using Classroom, and then compare paper and copy costs from the prior year to see how much of a difference it can make. You might even have a statistics or economics class run the monthly numbers to show the ongoing financial impacts of reducing paper usage in school.

Differentiation, Remediation, and Enrichment. You can post video tutorials for students who need additional instruction to master a skill or concept, as well as follow-up activities for those who quickly achieve mastery and are hungry for more. Because there is no limit to how many attachments a post can have, a teacher can easily provide a variety of resources to suit different learning needs. There are a myriad of ways to use Classroom to increase differentiation in your instruction. For readings, post links to articles with different levels of text complexity. For projects, consider providing resources grouped by reading level and other measures for students with varying needs.

Look to the Future. At the end of a course, a teacher can "archive" a class. By using this archiving function, the classroom is preserved as it was on the last day of the term. The teacher and the students involved in the class retain the ability to look at it anytime they like, though edits and changes cannot be made unless a teacher activates it again. Why is this important? A teacher may want to use past classes to help them construct new ones. A student may want to look back at an assignment or discussion for a refresher. There are any number of reasons a teacher or student might want to revisit a past class, and having the ability to do that is another reason Classroom is such an incredibly education-friendly product.

Writer's Workshop. Consider conducting a writer's workshop using Google Classroom. Students simply post their written work, so that peers can offer positive praise and constructive criticism. Some students may feel self-conscious about sharing their work, but collaboration provides them with the necessary feedback to improve their writing. You wouldn't have the members of a basketball squad do all their practice individually, nor should you have the members of your class do their work in isolation. Publishing and workshopping writing can open your students' eyes to new ideas and ways of writing they hadn't considered before.

ACT/SAT Prep. Not all students have the time or money for college entrance exam tutoring. Start a Classroom dedicated to test prep. Posts could include a question of the day, links to tips and tricks, practice assessments, and more! You could even use the integrated calendar feature to schedule face-to-face study groups and guest lecturers.

Project-Based Learning. In project-based learning, students dive deep into a given question or problem by doing research and investigation over an extended period of time. Google Classroom is well suited to project-based learning application because it allows teachers to curate resources and routinely check in on progress. Also, the various creation and content options give students choices in what information they share and how they do it. Because there are so many feedback and revision opportunities, students can continually submit and resubmit projects until they get it right. And, remember, not everything with a due date has to be graded. So, a teacher can assign a task associated with the ongoing project that has a deadline, but not necessarily a grade, attached. This allows both teachers and students to focus on developing skills rather than getting a grade.

Small-Group Work. Google Classroom has the potential to enhance small-group activities or learning centers, and keep a record of the work done during that activity. Simply post the procedure for each of the centers in the assignment directions, and attach the digital materials necessary to complete the task. Use the creation and commenting functions to make it truly interactive!

Guided Exploration. Design a WebQuest, Choice Board, HyperDoc, or other digitally driven activity, and post a Google Doc with the tasks you'd like students to accomplish or have the option to accomplish, as well as all the links to the sites they need to visit in search of information. Classroom can help anytime a teacher needs to curate a list of resources for students to access. All relevant links and documents can be attached to a single assignment or announcement so that students can find the resources they need quickly.

Take Advantage of Premade Templates. Google has a template gallery that includes tons of fantastic resources for educators. There are graphic organizers, templates for games like Jeopardy, and other useful premade tools created by education professionals. The premade templates even come with starred reviews so you can read what other teachers thought of them and how they put them to work in their own classrooms.

Parental Involvement. For very young students, send home the student login and password so that parents can help students log on to the classroom at home. You can post videos and pictures from school events, showcase student work, and add links to resources to keep students engaged at home. You can also use the classroom to share information about upcoming events or volunteer sign-up sheets with parents.

Avoid the Summer Curse. It's no secret that kids lose valuable information over the summer, but Google Classroom never stops working. Post summer reading challenges or links to DIY projects and activities students can do at home. You might even start discussions with incoming classes as a way to develop a rapport and start building relationships both with and among students before the school year begins.

Seminar Accountability. If you manage a seminar or study hall in your room, create a Google Classroom for students who are assigned to you during this time. You may not be assigning work to them, but you can help students manage their time and stay accountable by requiring them to post a journal entry briefly outlining the work they completed that day or week. Students can also use Google Calendar functions to let the teacher know if they'll be absent from a seminar or a meeting or event by indicating their whereabouts on a class calendar.

Go Mobile. Google Classroom provides free, user-friendly apps in both the iOS and Android app stores. The desktop version has a few more features (especially where teachers are concerned), but students can easily complete assignments, respond to questions, and post content from their mobile devices. Encourage students to download the app as another way of staying on top of due dates and announcements.

Connect Other Apps with Classroom. There are hundreds of educational apps and sites that have a plug-in connected to Google Classroom. This list includes teacher favorites like PBS, BrainPOP, Edpuzzle, Explain Everything, InsertLearning, Khan Academy, Newsela, Pear Deck, Quizlet, and Tynker—plus many, many more. Create assignments and activities with your favorite programs and connect them to your Google Classroom so everything stays in one place.

There are so many more ways to put Google Classroom to work for you and your students. Take time to connect with other educators who are using Classroom in interesting and innovative ways. Check the @GoogleforEDU Twitter account or the Google for EDU YouTube channel often for tutorials and new features. There are several Facebook communities dedicated to discussing best practices while using Google Classroom, and you can explore other social media networks like Pinterest and Instagram to discover how teachers are using Classroom at their schools as well.

Best of luck as you seek to establish Google Classroom as mission control for your course workflow. Remember, incorporating technology into the classroom isn't only a good idea because today's students find it interesting and engaging, it's important because tomorrow their livelihoods may depend on understanding how to use it effectively and appropriately. And, thanks to you, they will.

Acknowledgments

Thank you to all the wonderful people of USD 336 in Holton, Kansas, especially Melody Davies, Brenda Eubanks, Karen Ford, Debbie Harshaw, Matt Hundley, Stacy Lasswell, Jackie McAsey, Amy Oldehoeft, Shannacy Schimmel, and Tom Sextro for helping me with this project. Thank you to the team involved in the production of this book. Thank you to Google for creating incredible educational tools like Google Classroom and making them available free of charge for teachers and students around the world.

About the Author

Annie Brock is an innovation specialist and director of libraries at Holton Public Schools in Holton, Kansas. She has done extensive work presenting and consulting on educational technology and growth mindset. Annie has a master's degree in instructional technology and is a Google certified educator. She lives in Holton with her husband, Jared, and their children, Bodhi and Lila.